The Adhai-Din-ka-Jhompra Ajmer

(from Temple to Mosque)

(1151-1167 A.D. ; 1195-1230 A.D.)

Professor (Dr) R.Nath
M.A., Ph.D., D.Litt.,
(Retired Professor & Head of the Dept. of
History & Indian Culture
University of Rajasthan Jaipur)

(a) *The Nomenclature*

This huge building is situated in the ***Indarkoṭ*** locality,[1] at the foot of the *Taragadh* hill, inside the *Tripoliya*-Gate, on the western side of the ***Dargāh*** of Khwajah Mu'īn'ud-Dīn Chishti, at Ajmer. Several traditions related to its nomenclature '***Aḍhāī-Din-kā-Jhomprā***' (the humble hut made in two-and-a-half days) is on record[2]. James Fergusson's analysis is, probably, quite logical :

> "If it means anything, (it) can only apply to the clearing away of the Hindu temples and symbols, to provide materials for the erection of a magnificent mosque to the glory of the iconoclast conquerors and their self-exalting creed of Islam."[3]

---

1. This was originally a **large Temple-Town** which changed its face after the establishment of the Sultanate at Ajmer, c.1195 A.D. It is also called *'Andar-Kot'* (an inner fort) in popular parlance.

2. E.g. Har Bilas Sarda, *Ajmer: Historical and Descriptive* (Ajmer, 1941) (abb. *Sarda* hereinafter). 68-82 noted: "The name '*Aḍhāī-Din-kā-Jhomprā*' was given to it in the latter half of the 18th century when *Faqīrs* began to assemble here in the times of the Marathas to celebrate the *'Urs'* anniversary of the death of their *Pīr*, religious leader, Panjaba Shah (who had migrated to Ajmer from the Punjab) which lasted for two-and-a-half days, and *Faqīrs'* residences are *Jhompras* (huts)" (p.69). Be it as it may, it was not used as *'masjid'* during the course of *Faqīrs'* occupation.

3. James Fergusson, *History of Indian and Eastern Architecture* Vol.II (Delhi reprint 1967) (abb. Fergusson hereinafter). He visited Ajmer between 1835 and 1845.

Alexander Cunningham's comment[4] is a little different inasmuch as he allotted two-and-a-half days, not only for clearing the existing temples, but also for construction of the mosque, which was simply not possible. As its Arabic inscriptions, studied hereinafter, show, its construction was begin by Quṭbu'd-Dīn Aibak, *Sipahsālar* of Muḥammad bin Sām (Shihābu'd-Din or Mu'izzud-Dīn Muḥammad Ghorī), c.1195 and it was completed by his successor Shamsu'd-Din Iltutmish (1211-36), some time after 1229 A.D. Tentatively, the mosque may be dated between 1195 and 1230 A.D.

It is noteworthy that the two mosques, viz the *Quwwat'ul Islām Masjid* Mehrauli Delhi and the *'Aḍhāī-Din-kā-Jhomprā'* Masjid Ajmer were built contemporarily, commissioned by the **same patrons** and, most probably, built by the **same set of artisans**,[5] which is why the two are essentially similar structurally and ornamentally, though the Ajmer mosque is much larger.

(b)   ***The Site, Plan and Architecture***

The *'Aḍhāī-Din-kā-Jhomprā'* *Masjid* (Plate-1) is built on a high base (of roughly 20 feet=6.1 m height), which is obviously a precipice overlooking the valley. It is occupying the site of a large Hindu (precisely, Śiva) Temple, which was, most probably, built by the Chauhan (Cahamana) King Vigraharāja-IV (1151-67 A.D.) of Ajmer, as shall be studied

---

4.   "The only appellation by which it is now known would seem to point directly to the astonishing rapidity of its erection, and this could only have been affected by the free use of ready dressed materials of prostrated Hindu temples, I accept the popular name as confirmatory proof of the actual origin of the *masjid*, which is amply attested by an inspection of the edifice itself,' Alexander Cunnighham, *A.S.I, Four Reports for the years 1962-65* (abb. *Cunningham* hereinafter) Vol.II. 258-59. He visited Ajmer in 1864.

5.   Ibid, II. 260. The *Quwwat'ul Islam Masjid* Delhi was started by Aibak in A.H.587/1192 A.D, as recorded in the inscription on the eastern gate (R.Nath, *History of Sultanate Architecture* (New Delhi 1978) (abb. *HSA* hereinafter). Its northern gate has another inscription dated in 592/1195 (ibid, 9). Iltutmish (1211-36 A.D.), his successor, extended its screen, on either side, in 1229 A.D., after he had received the *Patent of Investiture* from the *Khalīfah* of Baghdad.

hereinafter. Its plan is of a single-quadruple (*Ekāngaṇa*) mosque, while the pillars and ceilings which make it up are spoils of Hindu temples. Exteriorly, it measures about 262 feet (79.86 m) square,[6] with bastions attached to the three corners. The eastern bastions (Pl.2) (on S-E and N-E corners) are built, roughly, on the plan of the *Quṭb-Mīnār*, with circular ribs on the three cardinal sides (W, S and E) and three angular ribs between them (also being the *tri-anga* plan of the Hindu Temple, with a *karṇa* and two *pratirathas* between the two *bhadras*). On elevation, these bastions also have such mouldings as *jādyakumbha* of the *pīṭha* of the Hindu temple. The south-western bastion (Pls.3-5) is quite different. It is octagonal in conformation and appears to have been **part of the original Hindu temple which was not disturbed**. It has all the basic mouldings of the *pīṭha* of the Nāgara Temple (beginning with *jādyakumbha*), as it had developed by the 12th century A.D. There is no bastion (or even a wall) on the north-western corner, which is in ruined condition. There is a broad stairway leading to the terrace.

The large court measures 200'×175' (60.96×53.34 m). It must have contained a *kuṇḍa* (tank) with stairs on all sides, leading down to water (for ritual-bath), which was later filled up. It was originally surrounded on northern, eastern and southern sides by pillared *dālāns* (cloisters), the main *pūrvābhimukha* (eastern-faced) temple being accommodated on the western side where, later, the *līwan* (sanctuary, prayer-hall) of the mosque was built. Cunningham's plan,[7] being its Conjectural Restoration, conveys the idea of its original structures fairly adequately (**Fig.1**)

---

6. *Fergusson*, II. 211. Cunningham's measurements are different : 272'6" (N-S) and 264'-6" (E-W), vide *Cunningham*, II.259 ftn. He found measurements also recorded in *Nāgarī* as 172 *hāth* and 167 *hāth* respectively which, at 19.0088 inches per *hāth*, almost correspond with his figures. Also see *Sarda*, 79 who recorded that there was a *Nāgarī* inscription of one Architect Dharma of Bundi, dated in V.S. 1462/1405 A.D. and these measurements were carved near it. It is impossible to verify these measurements physically, at present, due to wholesale encroachments and choking overcrowding of the monument like a bus-stand or a railway platform !

7. Ibid, II. Pl.LXXXIII; it has also been reproduced in *Fergusson*, Woodcut-375 on p.211 (which edition was published in 1876, after Cunningham).

Its northern side, built into the scarped rock of the hill, is entirely ruined, with living rock on its western, and a few modern buildings on its eastern end, just touching the monument. Bases of pillars have still remained *in-situ*, suggesting that there originally was a colonnade (*dālān*, cloister). The southern side has a continuous, rough stone wall (Pl.6), with deep niches given into it intermittently. They have receding 'lantern' (*kṣipta*) ceilings (Pls.7 & 8 respectively from E to W) and stone arches, which are closed on the external side, while those, on the internal side, on the face, are open on the court. These ceilings belong to the original temple, with which arches were used in early 13th century A.D. in accordance with the wills and whims of the builders. Temple material, including fragments of sculptures, is roughly embedded into this wall (Pls. 9 & 10). Bases of pillars have also remained *in-situ* on this side. In its centre is a gateway and a porch (Pl.11 with a simple but massive corbelled ceiling Pl.12) largely built with temple material which is also littered around carelessly. There are two other arched openings in this wall.

The main (arched) entrance of the mosque (Pls.13 & 14) is in the middle of the eastern side, with 4 series of 7/8 stairs each, owing to its unusual height. It has three distinctive features :

    (1).   flanking *jharokhās*, one on either side;

    (2).   prominent *gavākṣa* (ogee) of the arch; and

    (3).   a massive lintel (Pl.15) provided below the arch, ostensibly to support it.

The gate has a beautiful corbelled ceiling (Pl.16) and bears carved designs and Arabic inscriptions in *Naskhi* above the lintel, and in *Kufic* on the frieze. It is all stone-work. Original temple material, specifically, *lahara-vallarī* (wave) panels, which is easily identifiable, is used with the newly carved stones, and there is no doubt that the mosque builders tried their best to give the building a new appearance. The *gavākṣa* at the apex of the stone arch of the entrance gate (which is ornamental) is also a distinctive characteristic of the seven arches of the *maqṣūrah* screen of the *līwān*.

There are two modern godowns in the interior, one on either side of the gateway. These are full of fragments of **architectural parts and sculptures of a large Bhumija**

Śiva Temple which existed here, on this site, before its conversion into mosque. These extremely important relics are littered here, most shabbily, along with cement bags, bamboo and wooden poles, iron bars and other building material, making a mockery of our claims that we have an *Archaeological Survey of India* of the Government of India (operating under *The Ancient Monuments and Archaeological Sites and Remains Act 1958*); and a *Department of Archaeology and Museums* of the Government of Rajasthan (operating under the *Rajasthan Monuments, Archaeological Sites and Antiquities Act 1961*) for proper preservation and conservation of our archaeological and architectural heritage ! These have been studied in detail, hereinafter.

At present, only the *līwān* (sanctuary, prayer-hall) of the mosque has survived on the western side of the court. It is a large pillared hall, five aisles deep (wall to wall), with one row of 18 pilasters attached to the *Qiblah* (western) wall, and 8, 8, 18 and 18 pillars in 2nd, 3rd, 4th and 5th row of pillars (from W to E). In all, there are 70 pillars and pilasters in the *līwān*. Fergusson's Woodcut No.376 faithfully shows the plan of all that now remains *in-situ*, in the *līwān* (**Fig.2**). It has a screen of seven stupendous arches, three on either side of the central *īwān* portal, in contrast to the two arches (on either side) of the original *Quwwat'ul-Islam Masjid* Delhi. The roof of the *līwān* extends only over six front piers of five of the seven arches of the façade. Thus, it covers only 141' (43 m) N-S space of the *līwān*, beyond which, on either side, 54' (16.46 m) space is open. While the *Qiblah* wall is completely ruined on the northern side, the south open space (Pl.17) has seven pilasters. This and the overhanging brackets and ceiling slabs (as shown in Pl.10 above) suggest that there probably was a mezzanine floor in this south-western corner, or a subsidiary shrine with a double-storeyed *śikhara*.

The roof of the *līwān* is supported on these 70 pillars and pilasters (wall to wall). Internally, i.e. behind the *maqṣūrah* (screen wall), the mosque measures 141' × 40'-8" (43×12.40 m). It is, obviously, a patch-work and is **architecturally deficient**. The screen-wall is 11½' (3.51 m) thick and broken sculptures and architectural parts of the original temple are embedded into it, and also in the *Qiblah* (Western) wall, as was done in the *Quwwat'ul-Islam Masjid* and the *Quṭb Mīnār* at Delhi.

The Original plan, as conjecturally restored (upon archaeological evidence) by Cunningham (**Fig.1** above), consisted of five *utkṣipta vitānas* (circular corbelled ceilings) in the centre, on each side, flanked by one similar *vitāna* on either side and four at the four corners, there thus being 32 large corbelled ceilings in the original complex. At present, there are only 5 large and 5 small circular corbelled ceilings with which *kṣipta* (lantern) and *samatala* (flat) ceilings have been used on all their three sides, to make up the roof of the mosque which is, in fact, an extremely beautiful composition. The larger corbelled ceilings are supported on 8-pillars of the octagon, on a 12-pillars plan, with the help of massive pendentives and ornamental overlapping courses, bearing exquisitely carved designs. Each pillar of the mosque is built of three Hindu pillars (the lower ones without their capitals), fixed upright meticulously one upon the other, by ingenious system of interlocking. Thus, the present 70 pillars and pilasters are formed of 210 original pillars of the Hindu Temple.[8] It is all stone-work and there is **no true, radiating arch in the mosque**, obviously, because the builders were almost entirely dependent on spoiled temple material (Pls.18 to 26).

Both 'lantern' (*kṣipta*) and 'corbelled' (*utkṣipta*) ceilings have been used emphatically, while simple flat (*samatala*) ceilings have been associated with them, upon small spaces, subsidiarily. 'Lantern' is a method of roofing whereby beams or slabs are laid diagonally across the corners of a square or rectangle and the process is repeated in successive one or two tiers, so that finally only such an opening remains that could be covered by a single slab of stone (**Fig.3** for plan and **Fig.4** for section). The primary advantage of these flat ceilings was that there was no apprehension of any lateral thrust and no apprehension of any disruptive tensile stress. A large space could be covered by concentric rings (by corbelling, or overlapping courses in receding tiers). All these three types of flat ceilings are there in the *līwān* of this mosque, viz. lantern, corbelled and flat.

---

8. *Cunningham* (II.262), taking into account the pillars of the original cloister, surmised that there was 344 pillars, and "actual number of Hindu columns could not have been less than 700 which is equivalent to the spoils from 20 to 30 temples". Percy Brown, in *Indian Architecture* (Buddhist and Hindu periods) (Bombay 1971) p.114, noted that it has 235 pillars, each made up of 3 pillars of the original temple, "so that nearly a thousand pillars were used, representing the spoils of at least 50 Temples." It is quite likely that pillars from other temples of this **large Temple-Town** were used in its construction, they are so **different in size, form, style and designs.**

Not only the '*maṇḍapa*' form with flat architraves has been retained, in some cases, surprisingly, the original terrible looking '*kīrttimukha*' motif at the corners of the re-manipulated ceiling has also escaped the hammer of the iconoclasts. These exquisitely designed ceilings impart the interior an air of cool quietude, pleasant surprise and graceful beauty which quality of architecture is so wholly absent in the simple and austere brick mosque.

It is noticeable that the profiles and shadows, imparting a feeling of subtle mystery as they do, stimulate the devotee to the direction of an abstract deity than to such a simple and distinct phenomenon as *Allah*. With the magnificently decorated ceilings, harmoniously hanging over the contours of the sculptured pillar-shafts and capitals, this was unavoidable. **The whole rhythm of the interior** is so inherently in consonance with the spirit of the individualistic devotion that, it seems, the conversion of the Hindu temple into mosque only succeeded in bringing about a physical form, but the **spiritual atmosphere of the interior** remained essentially Hindu. It was not possible to alter it.

Except the *maqṣūrah* screen of seven arches, the entire mosque is built of gorgeously carved Hindu pillars, capitals, lintels and ceilings which together make up an extremely beautiful peristylar effect, as if **a Hindu soul lives in a Muslim body!** This is also illustrated on the terrace where the (five) large corbelled (Hindu) ceilings are externally filled up, and look like (five) hemispherical (Muslim) **domes** (Pl.27). Even this modest converted building, as early as this, marks the beginning of the **era of coalescence** of the two architectural styles, the art of line-and-colour with the art of mass and volume, which found its fruition in the age of the Great Mughals (1526-1658 A.D.)

While the original screen of the *Quwwat'ul-Islam Masjid* Delhi has only five arches, the *Aḍhāī-Din-kā-Jhomprā* Masjid has seven tastefully designed and finished arches (Pls.28 to 34) providing an extremely impressive façade to the mosque. Dimensions are almost similar. The central *īwān*-portal is a plain pointed arch which is 22'-2" (6.76 m) wide and rises to a height of 56' (17.07 m). Two arches, on its either side, are **cusped**, though they also belong to the triangular pointed type. The two extreme arches are also plain, without cusps. The three arches on each side are 13' (3.96m) wide, at an average. Curious oblong tablets, containing ornamental cusped arches and lotus, have been used in high relief on the spandrels of all arches, perhaps symbolically, as *talisman*.

Built of yellow limestone, these are trabeated or horizontal arches made up by corbelling (*kaḍalikā-karaṇa*), i.e. by overlapping courses, and there are no voussoirs. *Gavākṣa* (ogee) at the apex is their distinctive characteristic and it is more emphatic here than at Delhi. Three central arches have three bands of Quranic inscriptions each, exquisitely carved in stone, in incised relief (*carvo-intaglio*), in angular *Kufic* and intricate *Naskhī* styles : the first band rotates round the arch and the second one frames it, the two depicting Quranic verses in *Naskhī*, while the third one, rises from the bottom to the top, depicting mysteriously **elusive** *Kufic*. On the central arch, this *Kufic* band is continued on the top, making its second frame, with two additional broad bands, above it on the top. Perhaps, nowhere else in India, *Kufic* inscriptions have so exquisitely and so beautifully been depicted in stone carving. The credit goes as such to the native sculptors who executed them in stone, as to the calligrapher who prepared these writings on paper, in actual size. It is, perhaps, the finest and the most wonderful example of the fusion of such a typically Muslim design as **calligraphy**, with such a typically Hindu mode of architectural ornamentation as **stone-carving**. Technically, it is incised carving (*carvo-intaglio*). Letters are still razor-sharp and perfectly legible even after being exposed to Rajasthan climate for eight centuries ! In comparison, the Delhi inscriptions are much damaged.

Two turrets[9] of 10½ (3.18 m) diameter, with 24 ribs, alternately circular and angular, exactly like the plan of the *Quṭb-Mīnār*, surmounted the central *Īwān*-portal (see Pl.31 above) They are now ruined. Quranic verses were also inscribed on them horizontally. The white marble *miḥrāb*, denoting the *Qiblah* (the direction of the *Ka'bah* in Mecca), is built in the centre of the western wall, facing the central arch. It is also cusped and has *gavākṣa* (ogee) at the apex too (Pl. 35).

---

9.   They do not have internal spiralling stairway and, technically, they are not minarets (*mīnārs*).

Fergusson's comment on the historical and architectural importance of this screen of the Ajmer mosque must be quoted for the attention of the conscientious historians and archaeologists and, specifically, for the notice of those authorities of the Government of India who are liable for the proper maintenance, upkeep and preservation of our architectural heritage :

"It is neither, however, its dimensions nor design that makes this screen one of the most remarkable architectural objects in India, but the mode in which it is decorated. Nothing can exceed the taste with which the *Kufic* and *Tughra* inscriptions are interwoven with the more purely architectural decorations, or the manner in which they give life and variety to the whole, without ever interfering with the constructive lines of the design. As before remarked, as examples of surface-decoration, these two mosques of Altamash at Delhi and Ajmer are probably **unrivalled**. Nothing in Cairo or in Persia is so **exquisite in detail**, and nothing in Spain or Syria can approach them for beauty of surface-decoration.[10] Besides this, they are unique. Nowhere else would it be possible to find Muhammedan largeness of conception, combined with Hindu delicacy of ornamentation, carried out to the same extent and in the same manner. If to this we add their historical value as the first mosques erected in India, and their ethnographic importance as bringing out the leading characteristics of the two races in so distinct and marked a manner, there are certainly no two buildings in India that better deserve the protecting care of Government; the one (at Delhi) has received its fair share of attention; the other (at Ajmer) has, till quite lately, been **most shamefully neglected and most barbarously ill-treated.**"[11]

---

10. Obviously, owing to the traditional art of stone-carving ensuring a beautiful interplay of the '**Light and Shadow**' in the third dimension !

11. *Fergusson* p.214. Though his book was published in 1876, he made this comment between 1835 and 1845 when he visited Ajmer and this reproach was initially meant for the government of the British East India Co. The Crown took over in 1858 but, until 1947 when it passed on the sceptre to the Congress, it did absolutely nothing to improve its condition. During the last seven decades' time, since 1947, we too have miserably failed to conserve it properly, and **Fergusson's comment is as valid today** as it was when he made it some two centuries ago. We are still not ashamed, obviously, because we have not been able to know the historical importance of our architectural heritage, particularly in Rajasthan.

(c)   **Sanskrit Inscriptions** (Plays)

Two Sanskrit plays (dramas) were discovered in the *Aḍhāī-Din-kā-Jhomprā* complex during 1875-78 surface exploration. These were studied in detail by F. Kielhorn in 1891.[12] He recorded that among the papers of General Sir Alexander Cunningham, sent to him, he found rubbings (stampages) of two inscriptions, containing portions of two Sanskrit plays:

> (A).   *Lalita-Vigraharāja-Nāṭaka* composed in honour of the King Vigraharājadeva of Śākambharī by Mahākavi Somadeva, carved in 37 lines on a black stone slab 3'-5" (1.069m) broad by 1'-11" (0.58m) high; and

> (B).   *Harakeli Nāṭaka* composed by Vigraharājadeva himself, carved on a black stone slab 3'-3½" (1.025m) broad by 1'-11½" (0.60m) high, in Nāgarī characters of 12th century in Sanskrit/Prakrit.[13] (B) inscription is dated in the year V.S.1210 Sunday, the 5th of the Śukla pakṣa of Mārgaśirṣa/22nd November 1153 A.D.

Śākambharī Chauhans were śaiva and Śiva is the deity often mentioned in the inscriptions. In a scene, Śiva tells Gauri that he was pleased with Vigraharāja's *Harakeli-Nāṭaka*. Vigraharāja enters and Śiva blesses him.[14] This is an important reference inasmuch as it mentions that Śiva was pleased with the King's play *Harakeli-Nāṭaka* inscribed in this building which was certainly a **Śiva temple**, besides being a **Sanskrit College** where Sanskrit literature formed part of curriculum.

Kielhorn recorded : "Through the kind offices of Mr Fleet, I have received from Mr Ramchandra Dube of Ajmere, not only additional rubbings of the inscriptions, here described, which have enabled me to amend my readings in one or two places, but also

---

12.   F. Kielhorn, *The Indian Antiquary*, vol.XX (June 1891) 201-212 under the tile: 'Sanskrit Plays, partly preserved as inscriptions at Ajmer.'

13.   Ibid, 201.

14.   Ibid, 203.

impressions of two other inscriptions, one of which contains a new portion of the *Lalita-Vigraharāja-Nāṭaka*, while the other furnishes a new portion of the *Harakeli-Nāṭaka*. And it is only from one of these new inscriptions that I have been able to insert in the above proper title and name of the author of the *Lalita-Vigraharāja-Nāṭaka* which do not occur in the inscription marked (A)."[15]

This means that even in 1891, there were at least four broken slabs[16] of these two plays and, quite likely, there were many more pieces which Kielhorn had no opportunity, then, to read and record.

Kielhorn's article was published in 1891 which shows, obviously, that these inscribed slabs were found earlier, so that Cunningham could take their rubbings which were studied by Kielhorn in this article in 1891. But Cunningham does not mention these inscriptions in his *Report* on Ajmer for the years 1962-65[17] which shows that these inscribed slabs were not there in 1864 when he surveyed the area. As it appears, these were discovered later (after the publication of his Vol.II) between 1875 and 1878 when Repairs, Surface Exploration and, probably, Excavation were conducted here at the behest of the Viceroy Lord Mayo; their rubbings were made and sent to Cunningham, then the Direcotor-General of the Archaeological Survey of India; and were found among his papers after his retirement in 1884.

Sarda recorded[18] that repairs were conducted here in 1875-78 A.D. at the cost of Rs.23,128/-. Repairs, restoration and excavation were also conducted in 1900-1903 at the cost of Rs. 7538/- under the supervision of A.L.P. Tucker, Commissioner of Ajmer-Merwara.[19] These two figures show that almost three times expenditure was incurred in1875-78 in comparison to 1900-3, and the former was a much larger and longer undertaking.

---

15.   Ibid, 204.

16.   These black stone slabs are now preserved in the Rajputana Museum Ajmer, *Havakeli-Nātaka* on Nos.252 and 253, and *Lalita-Vigraharāja-Nāṭaka* on Nos. 254 and 255.

17.   A.S.I, Vol.II, 252-263.

18.   *Sarda*, 71.

19.   Vide the *A.S.I. Annual Report* 1902-3, 80-84.

He mentioned,[20] specifically, that "during excavations in 1875-76 A.D.,[21] six fragmentary tablets of polished basalt were recovered. Four of these contain parts of two plays in Sanskrit and Prakrit, *Lalita-Vigraharāja-Nāṭaka* on slabs one and two (which he briefly described) and *Harakeli-Nāṭaka* of Vigraharāja himself on slabs three and four[22] (Pls.5/55 to 5/58 respectively). The play is partly in imitation of Bharavi's *Kirātarjunīya*. Sarda confirmed the date 22 November 1153 A.D. He also noted that these inscriptions were engraved (i.e. carved in stone) by Bhaskar, son of Mahipati and grandson of Govinda (a favourite of King Bhoj, obviously, King Bhoja Paramāra of Dhar-Ujjain-Avanti), belonging to a family of Hūṇa chiefs who had been admitted into Hinduism.[23] This reference is important as, most probably, it establishes a connection with King Bhoja Paramara of Dhar (1018-54 A.D.) who had established there a Sanskrit College, much before Vigraharāja (1151-67 A.D.).

In addition to these four inscriptions which were also studied by Kielhorn in 1891, Sarda described two other Sanskrit inscriptions which were found at *Aḍhāī-Din-kā-Jhomprā* Ajmer. The fifth one is a *stuti*, i.e. invocation to various gods, specifically, to Sūrya (the Sun). It records that the Chauhans descended from the Sun and were ***Surya-vamśīs***. "The remaining portions appear to have been engraved on other stones which **undoubtedly still lie buried in the debris of the Jhompra**. This inscription is in pure Sanskrit."[24]

The few pieces of the sixth slab contains a *praśasti* (panegyric)[25] of the Chauhans of Ajmer, **giving their genealogical table**. It mentions that "Ajmer was made for his residence by King Ajaideva,"[26] meaning thereby that Ajaydeva established his capital at Ajmer. He conquered Narvarma (King of Malwa) on the border of Avanti (Ujjain). Later,

---

20.   *Sarda*, 75.

21.   It is amazing that this extremely important **Report** of the 1875-78 work has not yet seen the light of the day.

22.   Ibid, 75-77.

23.   Ibid, 77.

24.   Ibid, 78.

25.   Ibid, 78.

26.   Ibid, 78.

he bestowed his kingdom upon his son and reitired to "the forest of the sacred Pushkar."[27] Most probably, he was Ajaypal, the founder of Ajmer. It states further that his son humbled the Turks (Turuṣkas) and captured elephants of the King of Malwa, suggesting that Ajmer was, somehow or the other, connected to Malwa even at this early stage.

As it appears, the 5th and 6th inscriptions[28] are the fragments of the **Genealogy of the Chauhans**, others parts being still buried in the court. Sarda, therefore, remarked :

> " These inscriptions are of the greatest importance to the historian and it is hoped that Government will see their way to taking in hand **regular excavations in the Jhompra** with a view to recover, if possible, the remaining portions of these important inscriptions."[29]

Two small Sanskrit inscriptions were also discovered by Sarda[30]. They are *in-situ* carved on the lintels of the small staircases in the back (*Qiblah*) wall. One reads :

श्री विग्रहराजदेवेन कारितमायतनमिदं ।

(*Sri Vigraharājadevena kāritamāyatanamidaṃ*)

(This building was constructed by Śrī Vigraharāja Deva)
The other one has faded and simply reads : "made by the illustrious King Vigraharāja."[31] Obviously, these are from the **original Temple-cum-College** which was built by Vigraharāja-IV in 1153 A.D. and these are extremely important epigraphs.

Besides these, such names as श्रीसिंहलदेव and सिंहदेव are carved in Nagari on some stones. They may denote Simharaja (14th king of the Chauhan dynasty, c.1000 A.D.), or Simhaṭa सिंहट (21st king who ascended the throne for a brief period between Chāmuṇḍarāja (1038-63 A.D.) and Durlabharāja-III (1063-79 A.D.) which shows that materials from some earlier temples of this Temple-Town were also used in the construction of this mosque.

---

27. Ibid, 78.
28. They appear to have been preserved in the Rajasthan Museum Ajmer, *incognito.*
29. But nobody has moved an inch in this direction. First edition of his book was published in 1911 and second in 1941, but no excavation, at all, has been resumed on this site since it was abandoned **half-way** in 1903, or conducted anywhere else at Ajmer.
30. Ibid, 75.
31. Ibid, 75.

(d) **The Astronomical Panel**

Fragment of a red stone slab was also recovered from the site in the same sequence. It has two rows of divinities, carved in high relief[32] (Pl. 36). The upper one has six standing figures showing (from left to right):

1. काल (*Kāla*, Time deity)
2. प्रभात (*Prabhāta*, presiding deity of Dawn)
3. प्रातः (*Prātaḥ*, presiding deity of Morning)
4. मध्यान्ह (*Madhyānha*, presiding deity of Noon)
5. अपरान्ह (*Aprānha*, presiding deity of Afternoon)
6. सन्ध्या (*Sandhyā*, presiding deity of Evening)

with their captions inscribed on the top horizontal border of the slab over them, respectively. Only the last one on the right side, i.e. *Sandhya*, is female, all others are male human figures with *uṣṇiśa* as head-gear. These are **anthropomorphic forms of Kala denominations.**

In the second row are seven seated figures of *Nakṣatras* bearing their respective captions on the pedestal below them, (from left to right) viz.

1. माघ (*Māgha*)
2. पूर्वफाल्गुनि (*Pūrva-Fālguni*)
3. उत्तरफाल्गुनि (*Uttara-Fālguni*)
4. हस्त (*Hasta*)
5. चित्रा (*Ċitṛa*)
6. स्वाति (*Svāti*)
7. विशाखा (*Viśākhā*)

---

32. It is preserved in the Rajputana Museum Ajmer, vide No. 1/75/451, for which see *Catalogue & Guide* to the Rajputana Museum Ajmer 1960-61 (Part-1 Sculptures) (Jaipur 1961) p.31 & Pl. IX. The panel size is 1'-½'×1'×1" vide Ojha Report for the year ending 31 March 1916, p.2.

They have human bodies but cow or bull heads, sometimes with horns (Skt. *Śṛṇga, v. Sīṇga*). *Māgha, Pūrva-Fālguni, Hasta, Ĉitra* and *Svāti* (Srl 1, 2, 4, 5 and 6 from the left) are female figures, while *Uttara-Fālguni* and *Viśākhā* (Srl 3 and 7) are male figures. It is only a fragment of the original slab and, as seems certain, the remaining 20 *naksatras* (i.e 1 to 9 and 17 to 27) were also depicted in this complex which was, most likely, a college of higher studies in Indian Astronomy, Astrology, Mathematics and other sciences, as much as Sanskrit Literature and Fine Arts.[33]

While Navagrhas are commonly depicted in the Hindu temples, **deification** and anthropomorphisation of *Kāla* and *Naksatras* is a rare phenomenon and, in fact, this seems to be a unique example in the Indian Art. Such forms are abundantly depicted in the *Kīrttistambha* of Chittorgarh built by Maharana Kumbha (1433-67 A.D.). For example, images of the four *Vedas* have been placed on the exterior of the 3rd storey.[34] Anthropomorphic forms of *Śukla-Paksa* and *Kṛṣṇa-Paksa* have also been stationed on the exterior of this storey. The four *'Yugas': Krata-Yuga. Treta-Yuga, Dwapara-Yuga and Kali-Yuga* have been depicted on the exterior of its 4th storey.[35] Seasons as ग्रीष्म, वर्षा, शरद्, हेमन्त, शिशिर, and बसन्त have also been personified and their forms are carved in the interior of this storey. This art is conceptual and symbolic, and it is based on a sound **theory**.[36]

---

33. R.Nath, *Elements of Indian Art and Architecture* (Jaipur, 1986) 36-37 (abb. *EIAA*)).

34. For full details of this matter, see R.Nath *Chittorgadh Kirttistambha of Maharana Kumbha* (The Idea & the Form) (1440-60 A.D.) (New Delhi 1999) 119-21, and Fig.4

35. Ibid, 121 and fig.5.

36. This theory has been discussed and interpreted in R.Nath's article : 'Formalisation of the Formless in Indian Art' (Ajmer and Chittorgadh) in *EIAA* op. cit. pp. 35-42.

(e) **The Sanskrit College**

Sarda believed that the *Aḍhāī-Din-ka-Jhomprā* was "used as a college-house."[37] Later, he explained it specifically: "if we remember the design and similar inscriptions in the famous *Pāṭhaśālā* (School) of Bhoja which was evidently the **prototype** of the *Aḍhāī-Din-ka-Jhomprā*, also showing that the building was originally a **college building**."[38]

As explained hereinafter with the help of the large-scale temple material found here, it was essentially a **Temple** to which a Sanskrit college was attached subsidiarily, as it happened at Dhar (Malwa, M.P.) where King Bhoja Paramāra (1018-54 A.D.) also built a large Śāradā (Saraswatī) temple, to which a Sanskrit College was attached. Similar inscriptions were discovered there and these may be summarily studied here.

Lord Curzon, the most enlightened Viceroy under the British rule, visited Dhar and Mandu in November 1902 and "left careful instructions for a systematic scheme of conservation."[39] Consequently, the *Lāṭ-Masjid* and the *Kamāl Maulā Masjid* at Dhar were taken up for conservation. An important discovery, of more than ordinary interest, occurred in the *miḥrāb* of the *Kamāl-Maulā Masjid*. This mosque was built "on the **site** of, and to a large extent out of **materials taken from a Hindu Temple**," famous as Raja Bhoja's School. "This inference was derived some time back from the existence of a **Sanskrit alphabet and some Sanskrit grammatical forms inscribed in serpentine diagrams** on two of the pillar bases in the prayer-chamber (*līwān* of the mosque) and from certain Sanskrit inscriptions on the black stone slabs imbedded in the floor of the prayer-chamber, and on the reverse face of the side walls of the *miḥrāb*."[40]

These inscriptions were, in fact, hidden on the back of the side walls. There was no chance of removing the stones but, very ingeniously and laboriously, their impressions were obtained through the holes which were there.[41] "The finest inscription is engraved

---

37. *Sarda*, 69.

38. Ibid, 79.

39. J.H.Marshall's article on 'Conservation' in the *Annual Report* 1902-3 of the Archaeological Survey of India, pp. 17-18.

40. Ibid, 17-18.

41. The process has been explained by Marshall, ibid, p.18.

on a slab of black stone 5'-8"×5' (1.73×1.52 m) which was set up in the northern wall of the *miḥrāb*. The language is Sanskrit and Prakrit. There are **82 lines** in all,[42] containing the first two acts of a **drama**, written in praise of the last great Paramāra King Arjunavarman (c.1210-18 A.D.), the 19th in descent from the founder Upendra, and the 10th from the famous Bhoja. The remaining portion of this stone-inscribed drama has not been found. The drama commemorates in particular the King's victory over Jayasimha Siddharaja, the ruler of Gujarat (?)[42-A] in the neighbourhood of the mountain Parva-Parvata (*Pāvāgaḍh* in the Panch Mahals). The corresponding slab on the opposite side of the *miḥrab* bears a Prakrit inscription of **83 lines**, containing two odes (lyric poems) in the Arya meter to the tortoise (*Kachchhapa*) incarnation of Viṣṇu – **one composed by King Bhoja himself**; and the other by a poet of his court. Both slabs have now been fixed securely in strong frames and, for the present, are being preserved in the mosque. Besides the above, **eight other fragments of Prakrit inscriptions** were brought to light, one of which, consisting of **75 lines**, is stated to have been **composed by Raja Bhoja**. None of the fragments or of the more complete inscriptions possesses any date."[43]

There seems to be no doubt that several literary works authored by King Bhoja Paramāra (1018-54 A.D.) were inscribed here at Dhar in the Śāradā Temple where a Sanskrit College was also established. Vigraharāja-IV Chauhan (1151-67) appears to have emulated his great predecessor King Bhoja and he too, in order to patronise and promote traditional knowledge and learning, as much as for the sake of fame (*Kirtti*), established a Sanskrit College here at Ajmer, in the prestigious Chauhan capital which had then, in the 12th century, assumed National importance.

---

42.   The size of the slab and 82 lines of the inscription show that it is an extraordinarily large epigraphic record.

42-A.   Jayasimha Siddharāja (1029-1063 A.D.) was the most illustrious King of the Chalukyas of Gujarat who had their Capital at Anahillapaṭaka (अराहिल्लपाटक) (Anhilpatan or only Patan). He founded Siddhpur on the bank of the river Saraswati and built the magnificent Śiva Temple called '*Rudramāla*'. His *Sahastralinga sarovara*, with a thousand Śiva temples, was his famous architectural project. Obviously, the reference is to Bhoja who was his contemporary.

43.   Ibid, 18.

(f) ***The Arabic Inscriptions***

All other inscriptions in the *Aḍhāī-Din-ka-Jhomprā Masj*id are in Arabic, being verses from the *Quran*, *Hadīth* sayings, or non-Quranic Arabic prose, giving historical information.

(1) The earliest one is on the *miḥrāb* (which is built of white marble). Beginning with *Bismillah, Quran* IX. 18-19,[44] it records two lines in Arabic, reading :

> "Built............on 21 *Jamādī al-Ākhir*, in the year A.H. 595/1199 A.D. The Prophet on whom blessings be shed: Be speedy with your prayer before (its time) elapses and be speedy with repentance before death (intervenes)."[45]

Thus it records it construction by Quṭbu'd-Dīn Aibak during the reign of Muḥammad bin Sām, Shihābu'd-Dīn Muḥammad Ghorī.

(2) On the back (*Qiblah*) wall, immediately, under the roof, are carved two lines in Arabic, in *Kufic* script, measuring 21×6 inches (53.34×15.24 cms). They read :

> "(built) under the supervision of Abū Bakr ibn Aḥmad Khālū al-Harawī (i.e. of Herat) on the date *Dhul-Hijja* 596/1200 A.D."[46]

He appears to be the architect of the mosque.

(3) Two pieces of stone, measuring 4'-11" (1.50 m) and 4'×6" (1.37 m) respectively, lying in the courtyard of the mosque, also had fragmentary Arabic inscriptions carved upon them, reading :

---

44. For tr. see *The Holy Quran* (tr.by Abdullah Yusufali) (Lahore 1936-38) (3 vols) (abb. HQ hereinafter) 443-44.

45. *Epigraphia Indo-Moslemica* (ed. by E. Denison Ross) 1911-12 (abb. *EIM* hereinafter) p.15, Ins.No.VI, Pl.XXIV for facsimile; *Sarda*, 79.

46. *EIM*, 1911-12, p.15, Ins.No.VII, Pl.XXVII for facsimile; *Sarda*, 80.

1. Of the nations……. of the kings ………of the Persians, Shams-ud-Dunya-Wad-Din (name of Iltutmish with epithets) who ascended the throne.

2. Cavern of Islam and the Muslims, the Shadow of God in the world (*Zil-Allah fi al-'Ālam*).[47]

Thus, the part of the mosque on which these inscriptions were placed was built by Iltutmish (1211-36 A.D.) who completed the mosque (which was begun by Aibak). It is not possible that such long stone-slabs could have been used on the southern minaret of the mosque, as surmised by Denison Ross.[48]

(4) The Arabic inscription on the lower band of the northern minaret reads :

> "the Sulṭān of the Sulṭāns of the East Abū'l Muzaffar Iltutmish-as Sultani, the helper of the Prince of the Faithful, may God perpetuate his Kingship and rule, and raise for him his rank in East and West."[49]

(5) The upper band of this minaret has *Quran*, XLI. 31-34 inscribed on it.[50]

(6) Six verses of the *Quran* IX. 18-23[51] are inscribed on the outer band of the central arch (of the *maqṣūrah* screen). The Arabic text inscribed on its inner band reads as follows :

> "This building was ordered by the Sulṭān, the high, the just, the great, the most exalted *Shāhanshāh*, the Lord of the necks of the people, the master of the kings of the Turks and Persians, the Shadow of God in the world, Sham-ud-dunya-wad-din, the help of Islam and the Muslims, the crown of the kings and Sulṭāns, the subduer of the unbelievers and the heretics, the subjugator of the evil-doers and the polytheists, the defender of Islam, the

---

47. *EIM*, 1911-12, p.29, Ins.No. XXX, Pl.XXV for facsimile; *Sarda* does not mention these inscriptions.
48. *EIM*, 1911-12, p.25.
49. Ibid, pp.29-30, Ins No.XXXI, Pl.XXVI for facsimile; *Sarda*, 81.
50. *EIM*, 1911-12. p.30. For tr. see *HQ*, 1295-96.
51. For tr. see *HQ*, 443-45.

grandeur of the victorious government and the shining religion, the victorious and the lord of the land and the master of sea, the Sulṭān of the East, helped from the sky, victorious over his enemies, Abu'l Muzaffar Iltutmish, as-Sulṭānī, the helper of the Caliph of God, the defender of the Prince of the Faithful, may God raise him in every affair and render his proof conspicuous in every hour. And this was on the 20 Rabi-II of the year……..,"[52]

This long Arabic inscription is, in fact, an **eulogy** admiring Iltutmish with all possible epithets (*laqab*), giving the small historical information that this screen (*maqṣūrah*) was built by Iltutmish. Though the year has peeled off, it was certainly inscribed after 1229 A.D. when he received the Patent of Investiture from the *Khalifah* of Baghdad. This shows that while the main body of the mosque including the *Qiblah* Wall and the roof were built by his predecessor, the *maqṣūrah* screen of seven arches, along with the two minarets upon the central arch, was built by Iltutmish, who finished the mosque in all other respects.

(7) The following Quranic verses are inscribed on the two side-arches :

> XLVIII. 1-6 (*HQ*, 1391-92),
> XVII. 1-4 (*HQ*, 693-94),
> LIX. 21-24 (*HQ*, 1527-29), and
> XXV. 62-66 (*HQ*, 941-42).[53]

Thus, there are inscriptions only on the three middle arches, and the two extreme arches on either side have no inscriptions on their façade and bear only carved designs.

(8) The following Arabic inscription is carved on a lintel behind the second arch from the south :

> "During the time of management of
> Aḥmad son of Muḥammad, the Āriz."

---

52.   *EIM*, 1911-12 p.30 Ins, No.XXXII, Pl. XXIII for facsimile; *Sarda*, 80.

53.   *EIM*, 1911, p.33; *Sarda*, 80-81.

This thus records name of the *Daroghā* (Superintendent) of the work who was son of the Lord of Petitions (*Mīr-ʿArz*).

(9) Two famous *Hadīth* sayings are inscribed[54] on the entrance gateway :

> 1. "The Prophet said : Friday prayers are equal to an exalted kind of pilgrimage (*Hajj*); so long as he who says his prayers is in the world, the beneficent effect of the prayers is with him; and if he is in the company of those in Heaven, it is with him there."

> 2. "The Prophet said, for him who erects a place for the worship of God **with means righteously acquired**, the Almighty God builds a place (a similar house) for him in the Heaven."

Besides these inscriptions, such Arabic words as *ʿal-khāqāni'* (the King) and *ʿal-khalafa'* (the *Khalīfah*, being the temporal and ecclesiastical head of the whole Islamic world after the Prophet) are also inscribed on several stones.

It is noteworthy that inscriptions in the *Aḍhaī-Din-ka-Jhomprā Masjid* are **all in Arabic** while a few inscriptions in the *Quwwat'ul Islam Masjid* Delhi are in Persian, e.g. two lines inscription on its inner eastern gateway and one line inscription on the eastern gateway are in Persian, though most of the inscriptions, there too, are in Arabic.[55] The age of Persian began, in the right earnest, with such a great scholar of Persian as **Amir Khusrau** (1253-1325 A.D.).[56]

---

54. *Sarda*, 82.

55. For full details thereof, reference may be made to *EIM*, 1911-12 (ed.E.Denison Ross) 12-34

56. Reference may be made to R.Nath, *India As Seen by Amir Khusrau* (1318 A.D.) (HRD, Jaipur 1981).

(g)   ***A Compendium of the Remains of the Original Temple***

As stated above, the southern wall has 'lantern' (*kṣipta*) ceilings, fragments of architectural parts and sculptures, and temple pillars embedded into its structure, internally. Its south-western corner has a neat right angle, on the internal side, but, **externally, part of a temple has survived** attached to it. Five angles of its basic octagonal plan distinctly protrude from the south-western corner (see Pls. 3 to 5 above). Original foundation of this **S-W shrine** is intact, though stones of the *jagati* (plinth) have, some how, been disturbed. It has such horizontal mouldings (from bottom to top) as : *jāḍyakumbha*; *karṇaka*; bands of *ardha-kamal* and *lahara-vallarī*; *kumbhaka* of the *maṇḍovara* which is plain, without the usual *rathikās* and there is only a *śrīvatsa* band; *kalaśa* moulding (of the *maṇḍovara*); *antarpatra* (bearing *śrīvatsa-vallarī*); *kapotālī*; *jamghā* of the *maṇḍovara* which is also plain, having only a continuous band of *śrīvatsa*; *udgama*, made up of beautiful *panjara* designs; and traces of *khurachādya*.

These are mouldings of the temple *pīṭha* and *maṇḍovara*. Above them, from the point of the springing of the *śikhara*, there are vertical panels, alternately depicting *ghaṭa-pallava* and *lahara-vallarī* designs, exquisitely carved in incised and low relief. There is no trace of any *śikhara* and, instead, there appears to have been a first floor, over and above this ground storey, which was probably crowned by a mini- *śikhara*. This appears to be the south-western corner shrine (*karṇa-prāsāda*) of a large temple of *pañcāyatana* (quincunx) plan.[57] It must, however, be noted that the architect has taken the liberty to drop some of the *Śāstric* (textual) mouldings and to repeat others, in accordance with his own design of the temple; and that red stone has also been used along with yellow limestone in the construction of the S-W shrine.

This is a living part of the original temple which has remained in-situ.

---

57.   *Pañcāyatana* (quincuux) plan had a large temple in the middle and four smaller shrines at the corners of the *jagati*. However, this cannot be ascertained at present, without its proper conservation.

A portion of the wall of the original temple has also been incorporated on the external side of the southern wall. It has a different set of horizontal mouldings, suggesting that it was a huge temple, in which different sets of mouldings were used on different sections.

The following **ornamental motifs** have been used, most frequently, on this S-W shrine of the original Temple, on the southern wall and on the pillars, capitals and ceilings of the existing mosque:

1. ***Ghaṭa-Pallava :*** It is an ancient Indian symbol of plenty and creativity: "It is the emblem *par excellence* of fullness and prosperity, of life endowed with all its gifts, the full blooming overflowing contents of life are comparable to the plants and foliage luxuriating from the mouth of a jar (pitcher, *ghaṭa*) filled with the life-giving fluid."[58] It has been popularly depicted, as an auspicious symbol, in Indian art. Here, it has been used on pillars and vertical panels, in extremely beautiful designs.

2. ***Padma*** (lotus, *kamala*): It has been used here on lantern and flat ceilings, on pillars and also on *pitha* and *maṇḍovara* mouldings in *ardha-kamala* (half-lotus) bands. Symbolically, it represents the principle of growth, and denotes life floating on the surface of the creative water.[59]

3. ***Śrīvatsa*** : Like *ghata-pallava*, *padma* and *kīrttimukha*, *śrīvatsa* is also one of the eight auspicious symbols of the classical Indian Art[60] which have been popularly used for ornamentation in Temple architecture. It was deemed to be peculiar to Viṣṇu along with *vaijayanti*[61] which too is reckoned as an auspicious symbol. However, *śrīvatsa* has been used universally in Indian art in Vaiṣṇava, Śaiva,

---

58. V.S. Agrawal, *Studies in Indian Art* (Varanasi, 1965) p.43, vide R.Nath, *History of Decorative Art in Mughal Architecture* (Delhi, 1976) (abb. *HDA* hereinafter) 6-10.

59. *HDA*, 10-16.

60. V.S. Agrawal, *Indian Art* (Varanasi, 1966) p.159, vide *HDA*, 29-31.

61. T.A. Gopinatha Rao, *Elements of Hindu Iconography* Vol.I Part-I (Delhi 1968) p.25 : "*Śrivatsa* is a mark, a sort of mole which is conceived to adorn the chest of Viṣṇu in association with the *Kaustubha-Maṇi* which is a jewel," vide *HDA*, 29-31.

Jaina and other temples alike. It is represented "by a flower of four petals arranged in the form of rhombus, or by simple equilateral triangle."[62] It has been used largely on horizontal bands on the temple mouldings on the faces of pillars and other prominent spaces. Associated with adequate blank spaces, it also makes up an exquisite design in relief stone-carving.

4. ***Kīrttimukha*** : Though *kīrttimukha* has also been depicted on pillars, capitals and lintels it has been used most assertively on the corners of flat and 'lantern' ceilings. It is the symbolic manifestation of the terrible aspect of Śiva, according to the Pauranic mythology.[63] Literally, **'Face of Glory,'** it is a monstrous face "depicted symbolically in Śiva Temples, originally on lintels. Its use as an auspicious device to ward off evil became common and it was incorporated into decorative designs……..(it was also used) on the lower parts of the temple, inevitably on the threshold of the main entrance of the Hindu temple, whether Śaiva or Vaiṣṇava, from the tenth century A.D. onwards."[64]

5. ***Lahara-Vallarī*** (Wave design) : *Lahara-Vallarī*, in infinite variety of compositions, is **pure design, without any symbolism** and is used exclusively for ornamentation. Its designs are used as spiral or scroll in continuous series on temple door-jambs, lintels and pillars, on the horizontal and vertical panels; and are sometimes composed with *hamsa* (swan) *mayūra* (peacock) and *makara* (fabulous aquatic animal resembling crocodile). These designs are used for mural ornamentation on different zones and planes of the temple. It has no floral element at all, and is made up of infinite curves, twists and intertwining tendrils; it rises and falls like '*wave*' and moves forth with exquisite grace like a sinuous scroll, hence its nomenclature: **'*Lahara-Vallarī*'**. Its forms are crescentic, lines

---

62. Rao, p.25; *HDA*, 29-31.

63. *HDA*, 22-23. The Pauranic myth and how it was created, is narrated on its p.22.

64. Ibid, p.23.

serpentine. It is sometimes combined with a fabulous animal, preferably aquatic like *'makara'*, to retain its original wave character. At *Adhai-Din-ka-Jhompra*, however, it has been used most beautifully with *ghaṭa-pallava* and *kīrttimukha* both on horizontal and vertical panels.

As the relics discovered here, through the ages, testify, it was originally a Śiva Temple. A.L.P. Tucker, in his Report on 'Restoration Work in Ajmir' noted :

> "In 1902, a large **white marble *linga* was discovered in the course of excavation in the courtyard.** This confirms the Brahmanical character of the early temple, which has often been incorrectly described as Jain."[65]

This shows that the ***Śiva-Linga***[66] was buried there intact. The Turks would not have spared it and would have certainly broken it into pieces and, obviously, the *'Linga'* was buried by the *Pujārīs* of the Temple before its capture by the Turks. This testifies, beyond any doubt, that **this was primarily a Temple** (to which a Sanskrit College was attached) and it was a Śiva Temple where this *linga* was in worship.

This is confirmed by a large number of architectural parts and sculptures of the original temple, excavated here and stored, most shabbily, in the A.S.I. godowns in this complex itself.[67] These are fragments of the *kumbhaka* of *maṇḍovara*, *khuraçhādya*, *śikhara*, *samvaraṇā* roof of the *maṇḍapa*, *āmalaka* of

---

65. *A.S.I. Annual Report* 1902-3, p.81; *Sarda*, p.69 ftn.2.

66. Present whereabout of this *'Śiva Linga'* are not known: what happened to it ? Has it been exhibited somewhere or stored in some godown ? Or has this invaluable historical relic been lost to us forever, thanks to Archaeological Survey of India ?

67. It is with great difficulty that permission to photograph these relics could be obtained from the A.S.I. Our correspondence with the A.S.I. regarding antiquities stored in the *Adhai-Din-ka-Jhompra* complex, as also our correspondence with the A.S.I. for resuming archaeological excavation at Ajmer, is on record.

the *śikhara*, *stambha* and *śirṣa*, *uttaranga*, *utkṣipta vitāna* and *pratimās* and *mūrttis*, as follows[68]:

I. fragments of the *kumbhaka* of *maṇḍovara* (Pl. 37);

II. fragment of *khuraçhādya* (Pl.38);

III. fragments of the *śikhara* (Pls. 39 & 40); by and large, it appears to have been a *bhūmija śikhara* which was covered by *jāla-gavākṣa* design;[69]

IV. fragments of the *samvaraṇā* (stepped pyramidal bell) roof of the *maṇḍapa* (Pls. 41 & 42);

V. fragments of the main *āmalaka*[70] (*āmalasāraka*) of the *śikhara* (Pl.43) and a subsidiary one ;

VI. fragments of *stambhas* and *śīrṣas* (pillars and capitals) (Pls. 44 to 49);

VII. fragments of *uttaranga* (lintel) (Pl. 50);

VIII. fragments of *utkṣipta vitānas* (corbelled ceilings) (Pl. 51); and

IX. fragments of *pratimās* and *mūrttis* (images and sculptures) (Pls. 52 & 53)

All these architectural parts and, sculptures are remains of the original Śiva temple, which were discovered in this complex. Fortunately, five sections of the original western wall of the temple viz, the *Qiblah* wall of the mosque, built intermittently with them, the **former reinforcing and supporting the latter fillings structurally**, have also survived, leaving not even an iota of doubt about the existence of a large temple on this site. These can be seen distinctly on the exterior of the western (*Qiblah*) wall of the mosque (Plates 54 to 58 for sections A to E from N to S, and Pl. 59 for the whole wall). The

---

68. These fragments are lying, in heaps, in the two godowns of the A.S.I. (inside the *Adhai-Din-ka-Jhompra* complex) without any arrangement or order, **like lumber in *kabādi's* junk-shed,** and they had to be photographed as they lied there, and they could not be studied or photographed properly in the open space. Hence, there may be errors in their identification. It is also very important to note that 145 sculptures were acquired from the *Adhai-Din-ka-Jhompra* and deposited in the Rajputana Museum Ajmer, vide *Ojha Report* for the year 1908-9 ending 31 March 1909, pp.2-3. Is this a different and separate set of sculptures stored in the *Adhai-Din-ka-Jhompra* itself ? and have they been exhibited in the Museum ?

69. For *gavākṣa* and *jāla-gavākṣa*, reference may be made to *HDA*, 19-24.

70. *HDA*, 16-17 for *āmalaka*.

present north-south slope has much disturbed their elevation and the mouldings have gradually sunk into the ground from north to south so much so that while the uppermost moulding *khurachādya* is near the ground in Pl.54, the lowermost *jāḍyakumbha* is considerably above it. These sections have original foundations while the *Qiblah* wall of the mosque is only a later filling : hence the former is **structurally reinforcing** and supporting the latter. It was certainly for this purpose that these sections of the original temple were left standing, intermittently. This is a curious, albeit unique, phenomenon of the *Mandir-Masjid* relation, not found anywhere else.

(h) *Its Site is owned by the Hindu Deity*

After the Prophet Muḥammad emigrated to Medina from Mecca, in 622 A.D., he decided to build there a formal place of worship of his religion, viz. *'masjid'* (the place where *'sijdah'* = obeisance to Allah was performed). A **vacant** land was found suitable for this purpose. It was owned by two orphans Sahal and Suhayl, who offered it to the Prophet *gratis*. But he refused to accept the land for the purpose of building a *masjid* (mosque) on it without paying the due price/compensation for it and, consequently, a sum of ten *dīnars* was paid to them and the mosque was built on that fairly and lawfully acquired land.

This established, once and for ever, the **Principle of Legitimacy (*Ḥaqq or Ḥaqq-i-Allah*)** that land for the purpose of building a mosque cannot be acquired freely or forcibly, i.e. by barbarous means, but only in accordance with the Rule of Law, i.e. by paying due price or compensation (***qīmat*** or ***mu'avazah***) to the owner. This is indirectly confirmed in the *Quran* :

> "Never   stand   thou   forth   therein,
> There   is   a   mosque   whose   foundation
> Was   laid   **from   the   first   day**
> **on   piety**;   it   is   more   worthy
> of   thy   standing   forth   (for prayer)
> Therein.   In   it   are   men   who
> Love   to   be   purified;   and   God
> Loveth those who make themselves pure."[71]

---

71.   The *Quran* IX 108; tr. from *HQ.* 473.

That it is unlawful in Islam to build mosque on a land which has been wrongly acquired, without paying its price or compensation, and if a mosque is built on such a land, the *namāz* (paryer) offered therein is not legal and is not accepted, is maintained by several *hadīth* (traditions). One records that during the Umayyid period (661-750 A.D.), Muslims occupied a land which belonged to a Church and built a mosque on it. The Christians complained to Umar ibn 'Abd'al Aziz (717-720 A.D.), the *Khalīfah* who was renowned for his justice. On investigation, the *Khalīfah* found that the complaint was true and he ordered the mosque to be immediately handed over to the Christians.

This principle guided all legitimate, sovereign and civilized empires of Islam through the ages. We have illustrative examples from the Great Mughals of India (1526-1658 A.D.). Thus, Lahauri, Court historian of Shah Jehan (who ruled from 1628 to 1658 A.D.) recorded in his history, the *Bādshāh-Nāmah*, that a plot of land (*zamin*) situated on the bank of the river Jamuna at Agra, was selected for the proposed tomb of Mumtaz Mahal (viz. the **Taj Mahal**). It was owned by Mirza Raja Jaisingh (grandson of Raja Mansingh) of Amer (Ambar) who offered it *gratis*. This was refused. Lahauri specifically noted that keeping in view the religious injunction that no land could be occupied even for a grave without due compensation, and property from *khālṣah* was given to Mirza Raja in lieu thereof;[72] this is corroborated by two *firmans* which are record.[73]

Similarly, Lahauri recorded that when the Jami Masjid of Agra was proposed to be built just facing the *Hathiya-Paur* (the Elephant Gate now called Delhi-Gate) of Agra Fort and it was reported that some private houses were standing there, Shah Jehan ordered that these houses may be purchased by paying 10 or 15 times of the (market) value to the owners of these houses. Satisfactory compensation was accordingly paid and the land was, thus, **legitimately acquired for building the mosque**.[74]

---

72.   The *Bādshāh-Nāmah* of Lahauri (Persian text Bib. Ind. Series of the A.S.B., 2 vols (Calcutta 1866-68) (abb. *BNL* hereinafter) Vol.I Part-I, p.403.

73.   For full details see 'Mughal Firmans on the Land of the Taj Mahal' in R.Nath, *Medieval History and Architecture* (New Delhi 1995) 161-166.

74.   BNL, Vol.I Part-II p.252. For full details of this Jami Masjid see R.Nath, *History of Mughal Architecture,* Vol. IV Part-1 (New Delhi 2005) 441-457.

This shows that the Principle of Legitimacy (*Ḥaqq*) was followed right since the Prophet built the first mosque at Medina and ordained that a mosque could be built, and drafted for *namāz*, **only on lawfully acquired land**. Otherwise it was illegitimate, and prayer offered therein was not legal and valid.

The ownership of the land (and the material) of the Siva Temple, which originally stood here on this site, was vested perpetually in its deity, viz. Siva, who was consecrated in it. The Temple represented his body in which on consecration, he began to dwell and both the Land and Building of the Temple were dedicated to him. As the **Hindu deity is a perpetual minor**, he cannot sell, gift or transfer its ownership in any case, and **He is its PERPETUAL OWNER.**

This means that even after the Temple was demolished, its land remained, and **the masjid was built on this land which is owned by the Hindu deity perpetually.** He cannot be deprived of its ownership by any means. The *Adhai-Din-ka-Jhompra* masjid is, thus, standing on the land which is owned by Śiva and, doctrinally, it is not a *'masjid'*. No forcible occupation of a temple at any point of time in History, can legitimise a fundamentally illegitimate act.

Professor (Dr) R.Nath
(M.A., Ph.D., D.Litt.)
(Retired Professor & Head of the Dept. of
History and Indian Culture,
University of Rajasthan Jaipur)

'Tapasya'
7, Gulab Bari Enclave,
(Behind Asharam Chaudhary
Gulab Bari
AJMER – 305007 (Raj)

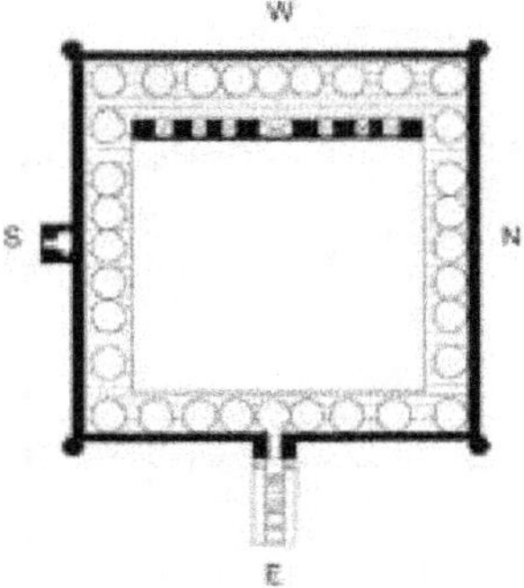

Plan of the Ardhai-din-ka-Jhompra
Masjid, (c. 1200-1215) Ajmer

Fig.1

Fergusson's Woodcut No.376 showing
Plan of Adhai-Din-ka-Jhompra Ajmer as it exists.

Fig.2

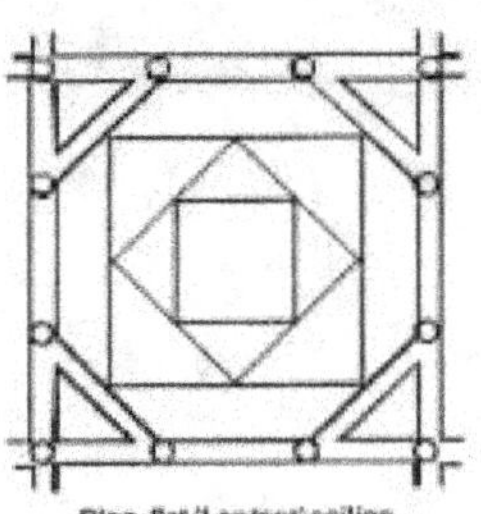

Plan, flat 'Lantern' ceiling

Fig.3

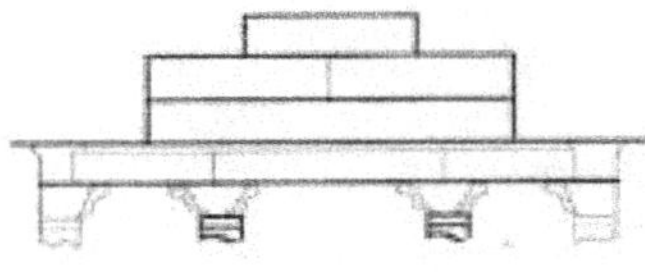

Section, flat 'Lantern' ceiling

Fig.4

Plate- 1

Plate- 2

Plate- 3

Plate- 4

Plate- 5

Plate- 6

Plate- 7

Plate- 8

Plate- 9

Plate- 10

Plate- 11

Plate- 12

Plate- 13

Plate- 14

Plate- 15

Plate- 16

Plate- 17

Plate- 18

Plate- 19

Plate- 20

Plate- 21

Plate- 22

Plate- 23

Plate- 24

Plate- 25

Plate- 26

Plate- 27

Plate- 28

Plate- 29

Plate- 30

Plate- 31

Plate- 32

Plate- 33

Plate- 34

Plate- 35

Plate- 36

Plate- 37

Plate- 38

Plate- 39

Plate- 40

Plate- 41

Plate- 42

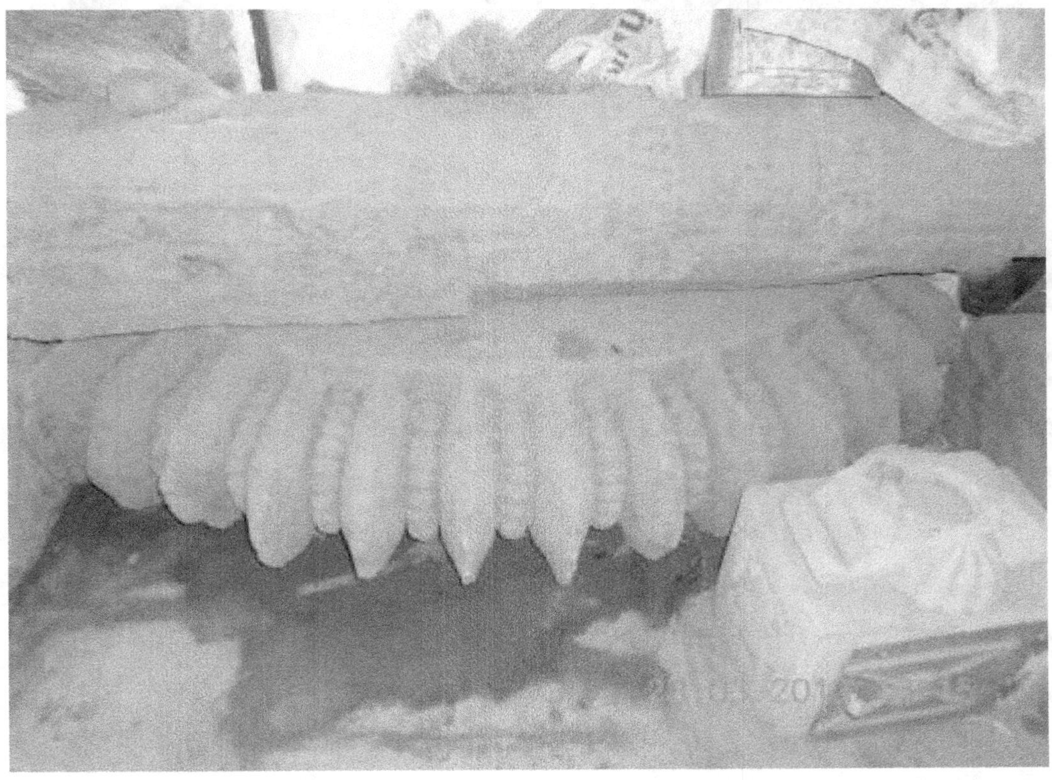

Plate- 43

Plate- 44

Plate- 45

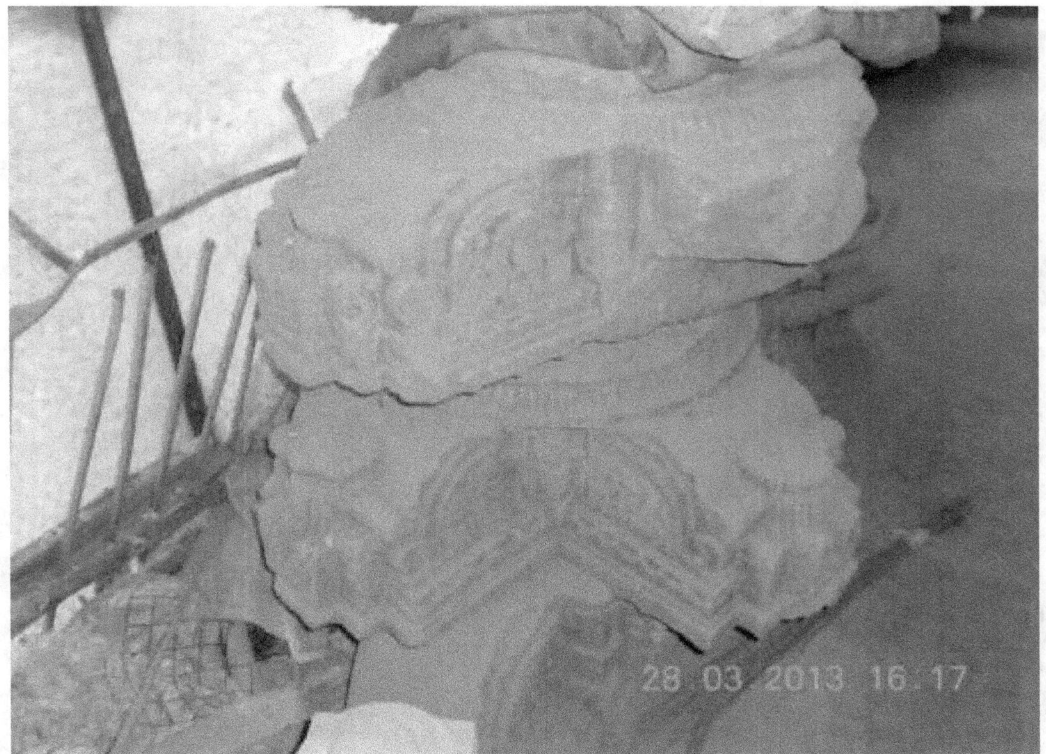

Plate- 46

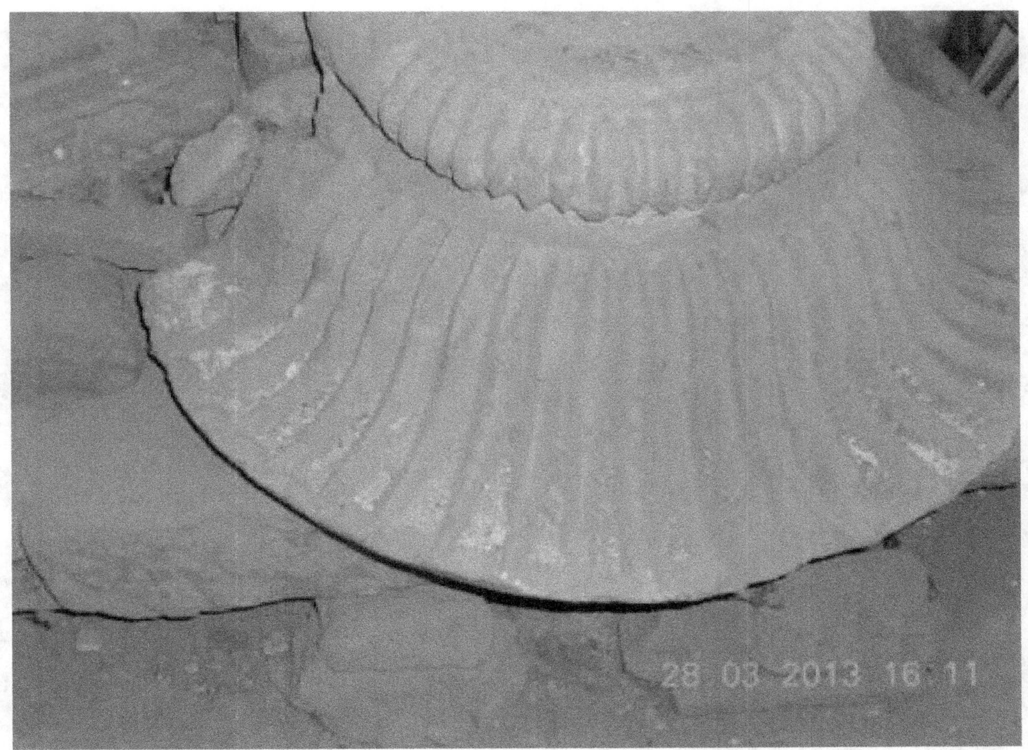

Plate- 47

Plate- 48

Plate- 49

Plate- 50

Plate- 51

Plate- 52

Plate- 53

Plate- 54

Plate- 55

Plate- 56

Plate- 57

Plate- 58

Plate- 59

*****